Cobweb Set

Written by Daphne Faunce-Brown
Illustrated by Lynne Byrnes

For Timothy and Caroline

Published by Studio Publications (Ipswich) Limited.
32, Princes Street, Ipswich IP1 1RJ

"BANG, bang." Cobweb opened one eye, saw that it was only seven o'clock and closed it tightly, but the knocking grew louder.

Grumbling to himself, Cobweb pulled on his dressing-gown and went downstairs. Outside stood a very agitated Wellington with only half his boots on.

"Cobweb, what can I do? My milk has been stolen again. It's the third day running."

“Come in, come in,” said Cobweb, quite forgetting how cross he had been feeling. “We will have a cup of tea while we plan how to catch this thief.”

Wellington felt better already. He hadn’t liked the idea of facing the thief on his own!

The friends agreed to meet at Wellington's house and to take it in turns to keep watch for one hour at a time. They started at half past ten, and at first all was well, but the later it got, the sleepier they became.

At a quarter past five, Wellington was woken by a shamefaced Cobweb who had to admit that he had dozed off!

The milk bottle lay empty; the thief had struck again!

"This is hopeless," said Cobweb between yawns. "This evening we will have an early sleep and then watch together from midnight."

As the clock struck twelve, Cobweb and Wellington settled themselves behind half-closed curtains.

At a quarter past two, they saw Whiskers deliver the milk. The moon shone brightly; they would have no difficulty in spotting the thief and they did not have long to wait!

At a quarter to three, a silvery shape slipped silently into the garden.

"Oh, no!" said Cobweb. "It's Bob Badger." He no longer felt in the least bit brave. Bob was well known for his strong paws and fiery temper!

12
1
2
3
4
5
6
7
8
9
10
11

The friends did not dare to challenge Bob. They watched him drink all the milk, sit back on his haunches, lick his lips and wipe his whiskers before strolling off.

Cobweb was thoughtful. “If Bob does exactly the same each night, and I imagine he does, I know exactly how to set a trap for him,” he said.

The following evening, just before midnight, Wellington completely covered Cobweb's prickles with fallen autumn leaves. It looked just as though Wellington had swept them into a pile.

"I do hope your plan works, Cobweb," he said. "Bob can be very touchy."

Cobweb smiled mischievously. "I don't think Bob will come back here in a hurry when I've finished with him," he said.

Whiskers came and went as before and didn't appear to notice anything strange. So far so good!

At three o'clock, Cobweb heard Bob drinking the milk. He then crept quickly and quietly as close to Bob's behind as he could get.

As expected, as soon as Bob had drunk the milk, he went to sit back on his haunches, but this time he landed on Cobweb's prickles! Twice as quickly, he shot into the air shrieking with pain.

Bob danced around the garden
moaning and rubbing his bottom!

When he saw Wellington laughing at him from the window, Bob was furious.

He gave the pile of leaves an angry kick, shrieked with pain again, and fled!

How the friends laughed as they enjoyed an early breakfast.

"I never knew Bob could dance so well," said Wellington.

"Perhaps he should give lessons!" chuckled Cobweb.